ANNIE JUMP
AND THE
LIBRARY OF
HEAVEN

Reina Hardy

BROADWAY PLAY PUBLISHING INC
New York
www.broadwayplaypublishing.com
info@broadwayplaypublishing.com

Cover art courtesy of Renaissance Theaterworks

First edition: November 2021
I S B N: 978-0-88145-913-5

Book design: Marie Donovan
Page make-up: Adobe InDesign
Typeface: Palatino

ANNIE JUMP AND THE LIBRARY OF HEAVEN
was first produced by Renaissance Theaterworks in
Milwaukee, running from 19 April-19 May 2019. The
cast and creative contributors were:

ANNIE JUMP .... Reese J Parish
ALETHEA .... Rachael Zientek
DR JUMP..Jonathan Gillard Daly
MRS GOMEZ/CHAIRWOMAN/DR FORD......Karen Estrada
K J URBANIK...Jarrod Langwinski

Director.. Pam Kriger
Stage Manager..Bailey Wegner
Technical Director .... Anthony Lyons
Scenic & lighting design..................................... Jason Fassl
Props Master...Jordan Stanek
Sound design & original composition ....Josh Schmidt
Costume design...Misti Bradford
Motion design ....John Fischer

ANNIE JUMP AND THE LIBRARY OF HEAVEN
was then produced by Rorschach Theatre (Co-
Artistic Directors, Randy Baker and Jenny McConnell
Frederick) in Washington DC, running from 19
April-19 May 2019. The cast and creative contributors
were:

ANNIE JUMP .... Vanessa Chapoy
ALETHEA ....Emily Whitworth
DR JUMP... Zach Brewster-Geisz
MRS GOMEZ/CHAIRWOMAN/DR FORD
.... Robin Covington
K J URBANIK..Aron Spellane

Director..Medha Marsten
Stage Manager... Linz Moore
Technical Director .... Anthony Lyons
Set design...Matt Wolfe
Properties design.. Alex Wade
Sound design.......................................Veronica J Lancaster
Costume design..Julie Cray Leong
Video design... Kylos Brannon

ANNIE JUMP AND THE LIBRARY OF HEAVEN
was subsequently produced by The Vortex in Austin,
Texas, running from 4 June-3 July 2021. The cast and
creative contributors were:

ANNIE JUMP ....Oktavea LaToi
ALETHEA ....Christina Blake
DR JUMP... Jeremy Rashad Brown
MRS GOMEZ/CHAIRWOMAN/DR FORD......Eva McQuade
K J URBANIK..Dane Parker

Directors .... Marcus McQuirter & Rudy Ramirez
Stage management .... Clarissa Smith
Assistant stage management .... Tyler Ortega,
Sarah Hogestyn & Amber Whatley
Technical direction..Chris Hejl
Lighting design .... Patrick Anthony
Assistant lighting design.................................. Jeremy Polk
Scenic design..Megan Kemp
Prop design .... Maggie Amendariz
Sound design..Johann Solo
Costume design.................................... Desirée Humphries

CHARACTERS

ANNIE JUMP, *13 year old science genius, female*

DR. JUMP, *her father, adult male*

K J URBANIK, *14 year old computer geek, male*

ALETHEA, *teenage mean girl who is also something else, awesome hair*

MRS GOMEZ, ANNIE's *teacher, adult female*

Offstage voices: VOICE OF GOD, CHAIRWOMAN, *and* DISTANT VOICES *can be prerecorded.*

DR FORD 's *line can be spoken live from offstage by the actor playing* MRS GOMEZ.

NOTE ON MUSIC

For performance of copyrighted songs, arrangements or recordings referenced in this play, permission of the copyright owner(s) must be obtained. Other songs, arrangements or recordings may be substituted provided permission from the copyright owner(s) of such songs, arrangements or recordings is obtained or songs, arrangements or recordings in the public domain may be substituted.

Prologue

*(A man [*DR JUMP*] stands at a podium.)*

DR JUMP: August Tenth, 2021.

(He checks his watch.)

8:03 P M…

This is the day, this is the hour, this is the minute

The minute we knew the Answer

Citizens of Strawberry, I am here to tell you…

We. Are. Not. Alone.

For the past ten years, I have operated Meti.net, a website that invites any alien intelligence monitoring our communications to make itself known via email, telephone or fax. We have been targeted by a number of jokers throughout the years, but because of the provenance of this communication, I believe…it is legitimate.

I hold in my hand a fax from an alien life form.

Do not laugh at me. This is a mind from millions of light years away that has chosen to speak to us. And I believe I have three minutes left, chairwoman, thank you.

(Reading from the fax)

Humans of Earth, we contact you in peace. We represent an intergalactic federation of enlightened species. Our name translates, in your Earth-tongue, to the Association of Stellar Serenity Healing Across Time Space.

Before humanity may join our federation, you must prove yourselves peaceful as well as intelligent. Dr. Jump, as a representative of humanity, we ask you to gather your small Earth-community at the following co-ordinates when the meteor display in your area has reached peak visibility. If all life-forms are present, displaying harmony, we will reveal ourselves to you. *(He stops reading.)*

"Displaying harmony." I believe the aliens wish us to prove our peaceful nature by raising our voices in song.

The co-ordinates are for Hamlin's field, just outside town. If you have any interest in a world beyond this one—I implore you. Come to Hamlin's field at the peak of the Perseids, at midnight, in three days. And you'll all see it. We're not alone.

(Thunder. Crackling. Horrible feedback. The lights go out.)

Scene 1

(In the darkness, adolescents cackle. The sound of feet running away.)

K J: Pete—yo, P T!

(More laughter, somewhere else.)

K J: Can you even believe this shiz? I almost peed. Pete?
(He enters, holding a flashlight.)
Where are you?

*(*ANNIE *stands up, seemingly out of nowhere. She has a work-light strapped to her head.)*

K J: AGGGGHHHHHH!
Who are you?

ANNIE: I'm the electrician. I'm getting the lights back on.

K J: Aren't you a girl?

ANNIE: Excuse me?

K J: No, I mean—

ANNIE: What are you, twelve?

K J: I'm a sophomore in high school. I'm a little short for my age but it's temporary. I haven't grown into my feet yet.

ANNIE: Oh. I'm a freshman.

K J: Also I skipped a grade.

ANNIE: Me too.
(She hunkers down and gets back to work.)
I've never seen you before.

K J: I'm new in town this summer.

ANNIE: And you're hanging out with Pete and those guys?

K J: We were pranking somebody. I'm, kind of like a tech guy—so my contribution was pretty crucial to the success of the project.

ANNIE: What did you do?

K J: I sent a fax to Christopher Jump.

ANNIE: Oh yeah. Dr Alien.

K J: I guess he's like, a legend in this town. Is he actually a doctor?

ANNIE: He has a doctorate. Psychology.

K J: Whoah. Legit? That's amazing.
Cause he's, y'know—

ANNIE: Crazy?

K J: Yeah.

So did you hear the name of the alien federation?
Association of Stellar Serenity Healing Across Time
Space.

(ANNIE *thinks for a second.*)

ANNIE: Asshats?

(K J *cracks up.*)

K J: I can't believe he didn't notice!
So, you're from around here? You're like, a
Strawberry?

ANNIE: I guess so. Can you do me a favor and make
sure this is grounded?

K J: Eh. Uh. I'm not really good with wiring.

ANNIE: I thought you said you were a tech guy?

K J: More computers. Programming, software…this is
so weird.

ANNIE: Hmm?

K J: You are definitely a girl, but—

(*The lights come on. K J shields his eyes.*)

ANNIE: What?

K J: Nothing. You're just surprising, that's all.

ANNIE: Surprising in a good way, or a bad way?

K J: Good way. Definitely a good way.

ANNIE: What's your name?

K J: Oh, shiz. I totally forgot. I'm not nonfunctional or
anything, just a little weird sometimes. I'm Kenneth
Jerome Urbanik. My friends call me K J.
What's your name?

(ANNIE *stands.*)

ANNIE: I'm Annie. Annie Jump.

Scene 2

(Lights shift as ANNIE *steps forward and addresses the audience.)*

ANNIE: Yeah. So all of that stuff was by way of introduction. I'm Annie Jump, and this whole story is about me.

I'm thirteen years old, I'm about to go to high school in the fall, and I've lived in Strawberry, Kansas for most of my life. My mom is from Chicago, but she's dead now. I don't miss her at all. I'm not mean or anything, I just don't remember.

It's not easy being a teenage science genius in a small town, especially when your dad believes in aliens. I try to take comfort in the thought that, even if he was totally and completely normal, no-one would like me anyway.

I mean, I have a 185 I Q, I got a perfect score on the S A Ts—last year, I put a hard boiled egg into orbit. Do you think there's anything I could do to prevent Peter Stockholm and his cronies from stealing my gym shorts, besides being totally and completely someone other than me?

Didn't think so.

Anyway, it might be packed with mouth-breathers and oil brats, it might have no Starbucks and only one yoga class a week—church basement, five P M, Fridays— but if there's one advantage to living in the middle of absolute nowhere, it's that Strawberry, Kansas has a dark-sky rating of two. And on the first night of the Perseids, when the moon is new…there's no city on Earth that can compare.

If you sneak out of your room and go out to Hamlin's field at midnight and look up, you don't see planes, or pollution, or buildings glowing on the horizon. You only see the stars, and the meteors and…

(Music is coming from somewhere, mounting in urgency. And then a whooshing wail like an incoming missile grows and grows. ANNIE points upwards.)

ANNIE: What is that?
What buttwipe is setting off fireworks during a meteor shower?

(An explosion. Green light flashes across the stage. ANNIE screams and covers her face. A small round object drops out of the sky and rolls to her feet.)

ANNIE: What the…
(She picks it up.)
…an eight-ball?

ALETHEA: That's mine, you know.

(A very pretty, nicely dressed teenage girl with a good deal of attitude has appeared.)

ANNIE: What?

ALETHEA: That thing you just picked up. It belongs to me.

ANNIE: Um—

ALETHEA: Do you understand American English? It's mine.

ANNIE: It came from the sky.

(ALETHEA gives her a look. ANNIE withers.)

ANNIE: Do you want it back?

ALETHEA: I just wanted you to know it was mine.
(She goes and sits on a rock and begins playing with her hair. Her hair is totally beautiful.)

ANNIE: Who are you?

ALETHEA: You can call me Alethea.

ANNIE: Alethea? Is that your real name or just something you made up?

ALETHEA: Do you think I would just go around making up a name like Alethea?

ANNIE: What are you, an oil kid?

ALETHEA: An oil kid.

ANNIE: The rich kids always have super fancy names. Clementine. Dashiell. Are you new?

ALETHEA: I just got here.

ANNIE: Well, look. I'm sorry to mess up your plans for tonight, but this is my rock. So can you just text whoever it is and tell him to meet you somewhere else?

ALETHEA: Meet who where?

ANNIE: Y'know, Pete Stockholm, or Darcy, or whichever boy you're planning to make out with. Oh come on. Don't pretend you're out here to watch the Perseids.

ALETHEA: The Perseids?

ANNIE: The Perseids—it's a meteor shower visible from Earth that comes around once every August—they call it that because—

ALETHEA: I know what the Perseids are.

ANNIE: Sure you do.

ALETHEA: I know everything you know.

ANNIE: You don't have to be embarrassed. We all have our areas of expertise. Mine is engineering and astronomy. Yours is. I don't know. Hair. Boys.

ALETHEA: I didn't come here to make out with some smelly teenage boy. I came here for you, Annie Jump.

ANNIE: Whoah. How do you know my name?

ALETHEA: Seriously?

ANNIE: You threw a pool ball at me. Are you some kind of stalker?

ALETHEA: *(Thinks about the question for a second.)* No. I'm the visual manifestation of a mindfurl of an intergalactic supercomputer built and maintained by a collection of the most advanced intelligent species in the universe.

(Beat)

ANNIE: You know what? Screw you. You are a terrible human being.

ALETHEA: I just told you that I'm not a human being.

ANNIE: It's not my fault, okay? He's my dad. Ha ha ha, Dr Alien, but I have to deal with that every day of my life, so you don't have to rub my face in it. I came out here to be ALONE. I came out here to watch a METEOR SHOWER. I didn't come out here to get made fun of by some popular fluffhead for something that I didn't even do.

ALETHEA: What makes you think I'm popular? Is it more the clothes, or the hair? I'm very proud of the hair.

ANNIE: I guess if you're pretty, you can get away with it.

ALETHEA: Get away with…?

ANNIE: Being a massive weirdo

ALETHEA: I'm not a massive weirdo. I'm a visual manifestation of a mindfurl of an intergalactic supercomputer. I know everything you know, and everything you don't know, and everything you're not allowed to know. I pretty much know everything.

ANNIE: Yeah, right.

ALETHEA: Try me.

ANNIE: I'm not as dumb as my father is.

ALETHEA: Try. Me.

ANNIE: Okay. Who discovered Cepheid variable stars?

ALETHEA: Henrietta Swan Leavitt, the Harvard computer.

ANNIE: What's Kepler's third law of planetary motion?

ALETHEA: The square of the orbital period of a planet is proportional to the cube of the semi-major axis of its orbit. Come on, Annie. This is high school stuff!

ANNIE: Fine. How do you reconcile quantum mechanics with general relativity?

ALETHEA: I can't tell you that. There's a slight chance you'll understand it.

ANNIE: Excuse me?

ALETHEA: I'm not supposed to reveal any truths or any information not currently known on planet Earth. No telling you the answers to the big questions, no giving you alien technologies. It's kind of like my prime directive.

ANNIE: No big questions, huh?

ALETHEA: Well, I can give you one.
Are we alone in the universe?
Hint hint.
You're not.

ANNIE: What are you even doing out here?

ALETHEA: I told you. I'm here for you.
I know everything about everything. But I also know everything about you, Annie.

ANNIE: That's creepy.

ALETHEA: I know what happened to your mom when you were little.
I know your Gmail password.

ANNIE: No.

ALETHEA: Stardate 403604. I know your middle school grade in intermediate Spanish. A Minus.

ANNIE: Stop it.

ALETHEA: I know your father used to read to you from *A Wrinkle in Time*. I know your grandparents sued him for custody when you were three and again when you were five, and again when you were seven. I know you were a muppet for your eighth Halloween party, yip yip yip yip yip yip yip…

ANNIE: You're a total freak.

ALETHEA: I can list all your father's court-ordered prescription meds. I know the only solo you ever sang in grade school choir:

(ALETHEA *sings. Her voice grows eerily large, as if miked.)*

ALETHEA: Somewhere out there, beneath the pale moonlight…

ANNIE: *(Overlapping with song)* Stop it! Just stop it—go away! Go away!

ALETHEA: *(Voice booming)* You can't ignore me, Annie. You're the one.
You're the Chosen One.

(Beat)

(ANNIE runs away.)

Scene 3

(ANNIE runs all the way home. She runs inside her room and slams the door. ALETHEA is waiting, smug.)

ALETHEA: If you're trying to get rid of me, you probably don't want to carry the probe around.

(ANNIE yelps and drops the ball.)

(Then there's a knock on her door.)

DR JUMP: *(Opening the door a crack)* Annie?

ANNIE: Dad?

DR JUMP: Is something wrong?

ANNIE: No.

DR JUMP: I thought maybe I could bring you a glass of sugar milk?

ANNIE: Sure dad.

DR JUMP: I'll be right up.
(He shuts the door.)

ANNIE: How did you get in here?

ALETHEA: I explained this.

ANNIE: You have to get out. I'm not allowed to have night-time visitors.

ALETHEA: Is that one of your dad's rules?

ANNIE: It just seems like a good general rule for a thirteen year-old?

ALETHEA: It's okay, Annie. It's not like he'll be able to see me. I'm just the visual manifestation of—

ANNIE: Stop saying that!

ALETHEA: I will once you get it through your thick skull. Can I use your internet?

ANNIE: *(Whispering)* Please get out. Please please please just leave me alone.

(DR JUMP enters.)

DR JUMP: Hi Annie. I have your milk. And the latest issue of *Scientific American*. It's got a thing about quantum entanglement and the firewall conundrum in black holes.

(ANNIE stares at DR JUMP, and at ALETHEA. ALETHEA winks.)

DR JUMP: I know you're mad at me. And I can even understand why you're mad at me. If you have anything to say you should feel free to say it to my face.

(ANNIE *doesn't respond.* DR JUMP *sighs, and hands her the milk.*)

DR JUMP: Here.
I know you prefer that I keep my work on the internet and out of the public space. If the communication, in its nature, had not necessitated public participation—

ANNIE: Dad—

DR JUMP: And I would say I'm sorry, but I cannot be sorry. I will not be sorry should it happen that in three days…well…it's simply too important. And I want you to know this has nothing to do with our previous discussion about my medications.

ANNIE: Are you taking them?

DR JUMP: I need you to not ask me that question anymore. It shows a lack of trust that makes you very hard to deal with sometimes.

ANNIE: Don't you want to keep me?

DR JUMP: Annie, oh sweetheart. That isn't something you have to worry about. You're my daughter. No-one is going to take you away.

ANNIE: Dad—

DR JUMP: Do you know what bugs me about lithium? I mean ONE of the things that bugs me.
It's SO OLD.
Only three elements were created in the big bang. Hydrogen. Helium. And just the tiniest bit of lithium. Everything else—from carbon to iron to gold—had to be cooked up epochs later, in the hearts of stars.

And yet lithium—one of the three oldest things in the universe—is something we put inside this—
(He taps his own skull.)
Really. It's barbaric. It's like doing brain surgery with a large rock.

ANNIE: Are you taking them?

DR JUMP: Of course I am, Annie! Have a little faith in me.
(He smiles.)
Three days. And I'll prove it to you. We're not alone.
(He exits.)

ALETHEA: Yikes. That is a seriously warped situation. Also, your dad's understanding of big bang nucleosyntheis is kinda un-nuanced, but what do you expect from a guy with a soft doctorate?

ANNIE: He didn't see you.

ALETHEA: I'm an auditory-visual illusion keyed to your perceptions. I'm invisible to everyone else.

ANNIE: How would that even work?

ALETHEA: Magic!
No, it's sufficiently advanced technology.
Your internet is kind of slow. I mean, I know this is the boondocks, but someone should apply for a grant or something. Look, Annie, do you believe me yet because I'm getting bored with this discussion and we have ground to cover.

ANNIE: Occam's razor. The simplest explanation is the best.

ALETHEA: Oh, quark.

ANNIE: You're an audio-visual illusion keyed to my perceptions. The simplest explanation is that I need help.

ALETHEA: You think you're crazy? Fine. Go downstairs and tell your dad to call the psych ward.

ANNIE: I can beat this. It might be a good sign. There's a thin crack between genius and madness. Maybe I'm even better at math than I thought. I just have to stay calm, and get to a confidential professional. I'm not talking to you, by the way. I'm talking out loud, to myself. It's totally normal.

Some idiot set off a firework during the Perseids and I found this stupid thing and now I have a fixation on it. I'll take it to school tomorrow, break it open in the lab, and prove to myself that it's just an ordinary piece of sporting equipment.

ALETHEA: Okay. Good luck with that.

ANNIE: In the mean time—
(She snaps her fingers—she has an idea.)
I made it for my radiation project at the last science fair. I know it's around here somewhere.
(She rummages around her room.)

ALETHEA: Seriously?
Doesn't the fact that you are considering putting the probe inside a lead-lined box mean that, on some level, you know I'm real? I mean, what would it prove?

ANNIE: Crazy Annie might need to be tricked, but Rational Annie is in charge.

ALETHEA: Look, this is completely unnecessary. I'll just sit there quietly and use the internet. Annie, come on. If you put me in there and it works, all that it proves is that I'm telling the truth—don't—DON'T PUT ME IN THE BOX! DON'T—
(ANNIE slams the box shut. ALETHEA disappears.)

ANNIE: Ha! What does THAT prove? Huh? Huh?
(Beat)

Oh my god.

(ANNIE *buries her face in her hands. Blackout)*

Scene 4

(Lights up on ANNIE *in the school science lab. She is decked out in full mad scientist gear, and she is working away at the eight-ball with some kind of electric saw of her own construction. Blue sparks everywhere)*

*(*ALETHEA *perches on the table, bored and annoyed.)*

*(*ANNIE *pauses, pokes at the ball with one gloved finger.)*

*(*ALETHEA *opens her mouth.)*

*(*ANNIE *turns the saw on again and goes at the ball with renewed vigor.* ALETHEA *rolls her eyes.)*

(After a minute, ANNIE *stops, pulling off her glasses and gloves and throwing them down.)*

(She picks up the ball and examines it.)

ANNIE: Nothing! Not even a scratch. Okay, different tack. A modern pool ball is composed of phenolic resin—which means it should be vulnerable to aqueous alkaline solutions.

*(*ANNIE *begins mixing chemicals.)*

ALETHEA: That's not what the probe is made of.

ANNIE: I'm not talking to you.

ALETHEA: It's a piece of inviolable nanotech.

ANNIE: And what compounds, exactly, are used in a piece of inviolable nanotech?

ALETHEA: Can't tell you. Prime Directive! Any alien tech allowed to enter a subject planet must be indestructible, inviolable, and innocuous. It can't arouse any suspicion, or be used as proof of our existence to any sentient save the One. That's you, Annie, B T W.

(ANNIE *submerges the eight-ball in a chemical bath. Fizzing.* ALETHEA *starts to gasp and choke, doing the full "melting witch" routine from* The Wizard of Oz.)

ALETHEA: It burns…. It burrrrrrrrns….

(ANNIE *watches avidly, glancing back and forth between* ALETHEA *and the ball.* ALETHEA's *chokes intensify and she keels over. The bath changes color.*)

(*Nothing happens to the eight-ball.* ALETHEA *pops up.*)

ALETHEA: Nope. Sorry.

ANNIE: I'm going to try another compound.

ALETHEA: Knock yourself out.

(ANNIE *starts mixing.* K J *enters.*)

K J: Annie? Annie Jump?

ANNIE: Yeah?

K J: I've actually been looking for you.

ALETHEA: Who's this geekwad?

ANNIE: Kenneth Jerome Urbanik.

K J: Present! I didn't know you were in summer school.

ANNIE: I'm not. You are?

K J: It's just the flipping foreign language requirement. I wanted to get it out of the way so that I can take more A P classes in the fall. Listen—about what happened last night—

ALETHEA: Whu?

K J: The whole thing was kind of weird, and I wanted to make sure you're not—not angry or anything.

ALETHEA: Tell me you're not mating with this human.

ANNIE: No!

K J: Okay. Cause you SOUND angry—

ANNIE: It was nothing, K J. You can just forget it.

K J: No—I wanted to explain. All that stuff I said about your father—it wasn't even my idea. It was Pete's idea, and…you know. This is a new town. This is my chance to make friends.
I think we're a lot alike. You're super smart. I'm super smart. We're both huge geeks and kinda weird—

ALETHEA: Is this his like, mutated way of hitting on you?

ANNIE: I don't know.

K J: So I just want you to know, if in the future, we're at school and we run into each other, and I don't say anything—it's not because I don't like you. I definitely like you. I've never met anyone like you.

ANNIE: Wait, what?

K J: It's just that—I can't afford to screw this up. I might never get another chance to be like—one of the normal kids.
So. No hard feelings, right? I hope you understand.

ALETHEA: Tell him he's a cowardly douchenozzle.

ANNIE: Yeah. Sure. I understand.

K J: Awesome.

ALETHEA: You're a cowardly douchenozzle! I don't believe this.

ANNIE: My father brings it on himself. He's crazy. It's no big deal.
(Beat. She continues mixing chemicals.)

K J: Aren't some of those volatile?

ANNIE: Thought you were just a hacker.

K J: I'm not ignorant, I'm just not very good with my hands. So are you running an experiment or something? I don't think you're supposed to be doing stuff in here without a teacher supervising.

ANNIE: I'm special. Mrs Gomez gave me a key. But I'm not supposed to tell people about it.

(Someone rattles the door.)

MRS GOMEZ: *(Speaking Spanish)* Hola Jeranimo! Estas ahi?

(She enters.)

Kenneth, you know students are not allowed—

*(*ANNIE, *mixing chemicals, creates an explosion.)*

MRS GOMEZ: Oh, Annie. It's you.

K J: Is SHE allowed in here?

MRS GOMEZ: Of course not. Jeranimo, I want you to go back to the Spanish classroom and wait for me, okay? I have to talk to Ms Jump. About the many many violations of school policy she is committing.

K J: For real?

MRS GOMEZ: Vamos, Jeranimo!

K J: Fine. Great. I was just trying to talk to her. *(He leaves.)*

MRS GOMEZ: Annie—

ANNIE: You said I could.

MRS GOMEZ: I said you could use the telescopes. I didn't say you could create an explosion on school property. That is a crime! If that goes on your record you can kiss your college scholarships goodbye—

ANNIE: I'm sorry, Mrs Gomez.

MRS GOMEZ: I gave you that key to encourage you…
because I think it's extremely important for young
women to become interested in the sciences.

ANNIE: It's just—

MRS GOMEZ: You're not the only person having a
crappy summer, okay? Do you think I want to be
teaching Spanish right now? I have a masters in
physics.
Your father is hard to deal with. I get it. But he's there
for you, and just cause he's a little weird sometimes
doesn't mean you get to act out.
You'd better give me that key back.

ANNIE: What about the telescope?

MRS GOMEZ: That is a privilege you lost.

(ANNIE hands MRS GOMEZ the key.)

ANNIE: I did everything right. It was totally safe.

MRS GOMEZ: I know you did, Annie. But it's not all
about you.
That boy who was in here…doesn't need your
encouragement, okay? He's already been banned from
the computer lab for doing some kind of nonsense I'm
not even allowed to explain to you.

ANNIE: Really?

MRS GOMEZ: I don't want him to get any ideas about
chemicals, especially if he thinks some girl can get
away with it, and he can't.
If it were up to me, Annie, you'd have a lab of your
own. And you'd get to do whatever you wanted in
it, whenever you wanted. Because you can do great
things, I know you can.

ANNIE: Mrs Gomez…what if I can't?

MRS GOMEZ: What do you want to know? You want to
know if you're smart? Annie, you're/ *(Smart)*

ANNIE: No! I want to know if I'm…like him.

MRS GOMEZ: Of course you're like your father. You're like everything that's best in him.

ANNIE: And what's that exactly?

MRS GOMEZ: Annie—

ANNIE: Every time he gets weird my grandparents take him to court.

MRS GOMEZ: I know. Look—sometimes the thing that makes you want to do something stupid is the exact reason why you have to always be smart. Does that make sense?

ANNIE: Not really.

MRS GOMEZ: I guess what I'm saying is that for some people it's hard, and for some people it's easy. And right now for you it is hard, and it's unfair, and I can't change that for you.

ANNIE: But what am I supposed to do?

MRS GOMEZ: I don't know.
Just…not this.
Now, I'm going to have to supervise you while you clean up. If anyone comes in, well. I was in here with you all along. But I'm only doing this for you once, Annie. Okay?

ANNIE: Okay.
(She starts to clean.)

ALETHEA: Poor Mrs Gomez.
She's so…emotionally invested in your progress.. If she only knew what I know—it would blow her squishy mortal brain.

ANNIE: Please shut up.

MRS GOMEZ: Excuse me?

ANNIE: I didn't say anything.

(She cleans off the probe and sets it aside.)

MRS GOMEZ: What's this? You learning pool?

ANNIE: I was just running some experiments—

(MRS GOMEZ starts tossing the eight-ball up and down.)

MRS GOMEZ: You should really learn pool. It's a great way to get an intuitive grasp of applied physics. Plus, you can make a little money when you need it. My uncle taught me, and me and my brothers used to go up and down the bars hustling people when we were teenagers. I could do all these trick shots—

(ALETHEA leans over and snatches the eight ball out of the air.)

(MRS GOMEZ looks down at her hand, confused that the eight-ball hasn't landed yet.)

(Then she looks up. As far as she's concerned, the ball is floating in mid-air.)

ALETHEA: Hey Occam. Razor this.
(She starts waving the ball in front of MRS GOMEZ's face.)
Woooooooo!!!!!

ANNIE: Alethea, stop it!

MRS GOMEZ: *(Panicking)* Annie, don't panic……get behind me……

ALETHEA: *(Overlapping)* So here's the question, Annie Jump. You see a teenage girl playing with an eight-ball. Mrs Gomez sees an eight-ball hovering in mid-air. Are you crazy? Is Mrs Gomez crazy? Or maybe, just maybe, is something else happening entirely?
(She walks to the middle of the room and holds the probe aloft.)
Mrs Gomez already thinks you're pretty smart. She's gonna think you're a genius now.

(The eight-ball starts to emit a pulsing, purple and blue sci-fi light as MRS GOMEZ *freezes and the lights in the classroom start to dim.)*

ANNIE: You're real. It's real. You're really out there.

ALETHEA: Oh Annie. I am all the way.
(She snaps her fingers.)

(Suddenly, ANNIE *and* ALETHEA *are floating in the black of infinite space. Stars twinkle in the distance. Every few seconds, a Perseid wooshes past.)*

ALETHEA: Annie Jump—welcome to the Library of Heaven.

ANNIE: What is this? Where did you take me?

ALETHEA: Nowhere. We're still in the classroom. This is your introductory multi-sensory media presentation.

ANNIE: Introductory to what?

ALETHEA: It's on screen saver right now. Hang on.

*(*ALETHEA *makes some swiping motions in mid-air. Something that sounds a bit like a D V D intro plays, and a voice booms "The Library of Heaven—and you!")*

(A supertitle, also reading "The Library of Heaven—and you!" appears. A meteor ricochets off its side and falls away in a shower of sparkles.)

ANNIE: Are you sure we're still in the classroom?

ALETHEA: I have the ability to put any image at all inside your mind. You haven't moved a step.

*(*ANNIE *instinctively steps forward and hits a chair.)*

ANNIE: Ow! What was that?

ALETHEA: I told you we're still in the classroom.

ANNIE: Can't you move it out of the way or something?

ALETHEA: The only object I can really manipulate is the probe, sorry. It's to keep me from going mad with

power and taking over the planet. Don't ask me how
we know that's a potential issue.

ANNIE: I need to sit down.

(She stumbles into the invisible chair.)

ALETHEA: Oh good. I'll start the presentation.

*(ALETHEA makes more swiping motions, and the
presentation starts. It is narrated by a "Voice of God" type…
whatever that means to you…and accompanied by fantastic
zoomy star graphics.)*

VOICE OF GOD: The Universe. 13.8 billion years old.
Unthinkably vast. Undeniably grand. And almost
entirely unknown.
Greetings, Earthling. You. Are. Here.

(The graphic zooms out to show the floating Earth.)

VOICE OF GOD: Here.

(It zooms out again—the Earth is a ball in the solar system.)

VOICE OF GOD: Here.

(Zoom—the pointer hovers on one arm of the Milky Way.)

VOICE OF GOD: Here.

*(Zoom—the Milky Way is a tiny swirl in a vast field where
galaxies are scattered like jewelry on velvet.)*

VOICE OF GOD: Does the size of the universe make you
feel insignificant? It shouldn't. You are important to the
universe. It needs you, almost as much as you need it.
But why should something like THIS—

(We zoom out into the entire universe—)

VOICE OF GOD: —care about something like THIS.

(—and back in with an arrow pointing at ANNIE.)

VOICE OF GOD: It's very simple. The universe cannot
see itself.

Looking out from your watery exoplanet you can observe ten to the 22nd power of stars. Of those stars, [redacted] possess exoplanets. Of those exoplanets, [redacted] are inhabitable. Of those inhabitable exoplanets, [redacted] have acquired self-generating bioforms. Of the exoplanets that have acquired self-generating bioforms, [redacted] have evolved species capable of looking back at you.

Somewhere out there, at this very moment, a young life-form fundamentally just like you is hearing a presentation exactly like this in a language you can't even imagine.

Greetings, Annie Jump, Chosen One of Earth. We are the Library of Heaven.

We are a vast brain, made up of signals pinged from star to star, of wandering probes exploring the infinite night. We contain all scientific knowledge. All culture. All philosophy. It is the one purpose of all life to join us in humble appreciation of the vast wonder of creation.

For every intelligent species, there is a Chosen One. A child of superior mind and determination who, according to our calculations, is capable of developing the technology of intergalactic communication, capable of achieving LINK-UP. Once that child is located, he or she is given a guide. The guide will point the way, but the chosen one must make the journey.

Annie Jump, the Chosen One is you.

Tell your guide whether or not you will accept the mantle. You have thirty seconds, beginning now.

(Begins to count down from thirty.)

ANNIE: Wait—what?

ALETHEA: Well? Are we gonna do this thang?

ANNIE: Do this thing? Do what thing?

ALETHEA: Become humanity's Librarian, of course. Oh, by the way, it's not official till I hear you say it, so—

ANNIE: *(Overlapping)* What?

ALETHEA: *(Overlapping)* —better say it fast. You've got like twenty-two seconds.

ANNIE: I can't just decide—I just heard about this. Thirty seconds?

ALETHEA: Eighteen seconds.

ANNIE: Become humanity's Librarian? A chosen one? I don't even know what all that entails.

ALETHEA: Entails? You want to know what it entails? It entails knowing everything about the world: geology, physics, mathematics, the stars. Devoting your life to the highest purpose, becoming the greatest scientist in Earth's history, and the secret most important human on the planet, learning every answer to every mystery that remains.

ANNIE: Oh heck. Oh heck. Oh heck. Oh heck.

(The countdown ends.)

ALETHEA: Annie Jump, Chosen One of Earth—

ANNIE: I serve the Library of Heaven!

(Blackout)

Scene 5

(Spotlight. DR JUMP is at a podium.)

DR JUMP: Greetings, citizens of Strawberry. I have requested time at this meeting of the Strawberry Elks to remind you that the last night of the Perseids is tomorrow, and we will be meeting at midnight to raise our voices in harmony, as per the instructions of the extraterrestrial communication.

Now, I have provided sheet music for the song we will be singing, it is with your secretary. If you are unable to obtain the sheet music at this meeting, I have filed copies with the Strawberry Public Library—excuse me sir! The noises you are making have left me in no doubt as to your displeasure. You do not have to throw things as well.

Yes, now—as I was saying, despite Mr Lambert's expressed opinion, I am sure the rest of you can appreciate the importance, the vast vast infinite importance, of complying with the communication. It is only a little music, but from a little music there can—there can and will come such great things. Mr Lambert, I have asked you once already, and we will have words about this in the coming age of splendor, technological advancement, and peace.

Thank you for your time.

Scene 6

(Lights up. ANNIE *and* ALETHEA *are sitting by the stargazing rock. Daytime.* ALETHEA *is wearing sunglasses.* ANNIE *is scribbling in a notebook.)*

ALETHEA: You're gonna need at least three units of that. Geology is still a weak area for you.

ANNIE: Rocks. I wanna know what really happens inside a black hole.

ALETHEA: Rocks first.

ANNIE: Is it cool, though? What happens inside a black hole?

ALETHEA: It is super cool.

*(*ANNIE *grins and goes back to her notebook. After a beat)*

ANNIE: Why does it have to be a kid? The Chosen One, I mean? I mean, there are grown-ups who are actually looking for you guys—not just my dad, but legit scientists.

ALETHEA: Okay, thought experiment. Say I go roll up to Jill Tarter, and I'm like, "Yo! Alien intelligence here!" What happens next?

ANNIE: I don't know.

ALETHEA: What happens if she tells somebody?

ANNIE: Um—it's the biggest media story ever, and everyone freaks out, and probably sets off some bombs or something?

ALETHEA: What happens if YOU tell somebody?

ANNIE: They laugh at me.

ALETHEA: Exactly. Plus, we get you young we can mold you into whatever we want.

ANNIE: So, you won't tell me the answer to any big questions.

ALETHEA: Not won't. Can't. It's against my programming. It'd be even harder than letting another person see me.

ANNIE: Can you tell me if I'm on the right track?

ALETHEA: That's kind of a grey area.

ANNIE: Okay, so unified field theory—

ALETHEA: Ew…

ANNIE: I just want to know if quantum mechanics can be reconciled with general relativity!

ALETHEA: It's cute that you think that's even your problem.

ANNIE: String theory? Is string theory provable?

ALETHEA: O M G you're adorable.

ANNIE: Is it remotely close? On the right track?

(ALETHEA *dissolves into giggles.*)

ANNIE: I'm guessing this qualifies as a no.

ALETHEA: Little vibrating donuts!

ANNIE: Shhh—someone's coming.

ALETHEA: I don't need to shush. I'm magic.

(K J *approaches the stone. He does that dorky thing where he throws a Frisbee and just pretends he's coming over to retrieve it.*)

K J: Hey.

ANNIE: Hey.

ALETHEA: *(Silly voice)* Heyyyyyy.

K J: Who are you talking to?

ANNIE: My imaginary friend.

K J: Are you a math genius?

(K J *laughs at his own joke. No-one else does.*)

K J: You know, like in that old movie where he talks to the…never mind. You always have the eight-ball. Is it lucky?

ALETHEA: Tell douchenozzle there's no such thing as luck.

ANNIE: No, I'm just thinking about learning to play pool. It gives you a great intuitive grasp of Newtonian physics.

K J: Mind if I sit down?

ALETHEA: Um, yes?

ANNIE: I guess not.

K J: This is a pretty great rock. Prettty great—at night it'd be perfect for seeing stars. Did you know that we're all made of stars? Yeah—the big bang only made helium and hydrogen and a scootch of lithium— everything else had to be cooked up through astral nucleosynthesis…

(ALETHEA *makes a "shut it" gesture.* K J *continues talking, but silently. She leans over and hisses in* ANNIE's *ear.*)

ALETHEA: Okay. I'll tell you what's happening now. You are being pushed around by someone who thinks he is smarter than you but is actually less smart. And you are just sitting there and taking it. You get that, Chosen One? This does not bode well for your career in the sciences.

ANNIE: But—

ALETHEA: He's mouthing off like he's the first person to watch *Nova*, he played a really mean prank on your dad, and he's not even cute. Why are you talking to him?

(ALETHEA *makes another gesture and* K J *becomes audible again.*)

K J: It goes hydrogen helium carbon—wait no—hydrogen helium— Wait, no—helium—

ANNIE: Shut up! Shut up!

K J: But I—

ANNIE: JUST PLEASE STOP TALKING.
First of all, stop screwing up the curve of binding energy.
Second of all, why do you think your crappy explanation of nucleosynthesis is going to impress me? Why do you think you can use science I already know as a pickup line?
And even if that did impress me, which it doesn't, and even if you were cute, which you're not, you are not a good person. You are being really, really, really mean. To my father. Not to some rando, but to my dad. And it wasn't even your idea. You're weak. You're a follower, and you've got no freakin' empathy.
And let me tell you something about Dr Alien, okay? He might be crazy, but he's not a cynic. He's willing

to believe in something bigger than himself. And that makes him closer to greatness than you.

You. Will. Never. Be. Anything. Kenneth Jerome Urbanik.

So why don't you run to your little friends, and come up with more little schemes to make Peter Stockholm giggle. I have real work.

(K J *gets up*.)

K J: Okay yeah, I can take a hint.

(*Beat*)

You're wrong about me, you know.

ANNIE: Yeah? Where's the evidence.

K J: Right. Well. I'll let you—

Okay.

(K J *exits. Beat*)

ALETHEA: Oooooooo. That was brutal. Are you sure you didn't…

ANNIE: Alethea, I'm thirteen.

Can we please stop talking about K J Urbanik?

ALETHEA: Okay, so A P Physics—

ANNIE: I can't take that till my sophomore year.

ALETHEA: Why not?

ANNIE: Strawberry High isn't offering it till then. Mrs Gomez can only teach so many hours.

ALETHEA: Ohhhh… Did I forget to say this part?

ANNIE: What?

ALETHEA: I could have sworn I said it but maybe it seemed so obvious to me that I thought it could go unsaid.

ANNIE: What?

ALETHEA: You're not going to Strawberry High.

ANNIE: But it's the only high school within a twenty-five mile radius.

ALETHEA: Not in Chicago.

(Beat)

ANNIE: No.

ALETHEA: What—did you think you were going to stay in Strawberry forever? Sitting on this rock and telling your dad to take his pills?

ANNIE: I'll leave when I go to college.

ALETHEA: By then it'll be too late. Look honey, we've run the numbers. If you're gonna be the Chosen One, you've gotta follow the Chosen One program.

ANNIE: Where am I supposed to live?

ALETHEA: With your grandparents, obviously.

ANNIE: My mom's folks?

ALETHEA: They want you, you want an education. It's like, a mathematically perfect solution.

ANNIE: We haven't talked to them in years. They hate us—

ALETHEA: Correction. They hate your dad. And they'd take you away from him in a hot millisecond. They've already served him with papers for like their fourth custody attempt.

ANNIE: What?

ALETHEA: Oh, didn't he tell you? The Demonstration of Harmony made it into the local paper, which means it made it into the world wide "information superhighway", which means anyone on Earth can know just how far your dad has driven into crazyville...
O M G—this is about him, isn't it? You want to stay because of him.

(She tilts her head)
Calculating.

ANNIE: Calculating? What are you calculating?

ALETHEA: I've just processed some RIDICULOUS new information, and I need to run the numbers on how it affects our lives.

ANNIE: Stop doing that! Stop!

ALETHEA: Humans make choices. Humans decide what's most important to them. If you stay here for HIM, Annie, he is going to hold you back, you are never going to leave the ground.
And how do you know your dad doesn't want you to go, huh? What do you think he'd rather have—his daughter around all the time or a direct link to the Library of Heaven?

ANNIE: I won't do it.

ALETHEA: Um, what?

ANNIE: I'm not going to suddenly move to Chicago just because you tell me to. It's not about my dad, it's not about any one thing. It's a…it's a constellation of factors, and I won't do it.

ALETHEA: Okay.
(She leans over and grabs the probe.)
You want out, girl? Say the word, and you're out.

ANNIE: Out?

ALETHEA: Yeah, *out*. Shrugging off the mantle, No Longer the Chosen One of Earth. No guide, no destiny, no link-up, no human members of the Library not now and not ever, and it will all be because of you.

ANNIE: Don't say that.

ALETHEA: If we're gonnna have you, we have to have you one hundred percent. Do you want to serve the Library? Yes or no?

ANNIE: *(Quiet)* Yes.

(ALETHEA *puts the pool ball into* ANNIE'*s hand:*)

ALETHEA: Then I need you to go home and make a call.

ANNIE: It's not fair.

ALETHEA: Girl, who said anything about fair? Do you really think we can do this without making some sacrifices?

ANNIE: Who's we?

ALETHEA: Say that again?

ANNIE: Seems to me like I make all the sacrifices and you get everything you / want—

ALETHEA: Shut your mouth, Annie Jump.
My whole existence is a sacrifice.
(Beat)
You don't want to leave your home. I get that. My home used to be the universe.
I was a part of the Library. I knew everything. I could go everywhere. I ran along the nerves of the galaxies. I was never alone.
And then they split me off. They made me an entity onto myself, and they boxed me up and shipped me to you. Now I am separate from the Universe, and I can never, ever, ever go back. Not unless you send me back.
So believe me, Annie, no-one is more invested in your success than I am. Not even you.
(Beat)

ANNIE: Chicago has a dark-sky rating of nine.
How am I supposed to tell him?

ALETHEA: I was a thought in the mind of god. Now I'm a toy. I didn't have a choice.
You do.

Scene 7

(DR JUMP *sits in his home office, surrounded by papers, typing maniacally.*)

(*There is a knock.*)

(*He doesn't respond.*)

(K J *enters, slowly.*)

K J: Dr Jump?

(DR JUMP *starts and turns.*)

DR JUMP: Young man! Young man young man young man. You are here. Excellent. Excellent. Thank you for being here on time.

K J: Uh—

DR JUMP: Come come come come come.

K J: I didn't know I made an appointment—

DR JUMP: You are here for the sheet music, yes? Or do you already have sheet music? It doesn't matter. It is useful to have extras. Here. Distribute these to all the block captains in your precinct.

K J: I don't know what a block captain is.

DR JUMP: But you ARE the precinct admiral?

K J: Definitely not.

DR JUMP: Curious. Curious. No matter. You can still be a part of the endeavor. We need all the help we can get.

K J: Are you talking about the—um the singing thing. For the aliens?

DR JUMP: It's the last night of the Perseids, is it not?

K J: Yeah—about that—

DR JUMP: It is so good to see young people taking an interest in the future of our species. In your future. My own daughter—she is unusually smart, fantastically bright, but she has a curious blind spot when it comes to SETI, almost a prejudice—

K J: Dr Jump!
I'm not here about the singing thing. I'm not doing it. Frankly, I don't think anyone is doing it.

DR JUMP: Then why are you here?

K J: Because I did something wrong, and I'm trying to make it right.
Before this whole thing goes any further.
Dr Jump, you should cancel the Perseids.
The fax from the aliens was a hoax.
Everyone knows it. Everyone in town is laughing at you.
You're the only one who believes.

DR JUMP: Nonsense. I've been receiving letters of support every day.
And the provenance of the fax is quite believable—I wouldn't expect you to understand, but—

K J: It's a hoax! A trick! A prank. It's just some assholes making fun of you—

DR JUMP: You have no proof of that.

K J: Actually, yeah. I do.
(He takes out his phone, and presses a couple of buttons.)

(The fax machine whirs to life.)

(It spits out a piece of paper.)

(DR JUMP takes it, reads it.)

(Sits down heavily in his chair.)

K J: I'm sorry.

I'm really, really sorry.
(*He exits.*)

(DR JUMP *sits and stares at the paper.*)

(*After a moment,* ANNIE *enters.*)

ANNIE: Daddy?
Was someone just here?

DR JUMP: Ah. Yes. He…he came about the Demonstration of Harmony.

ANNIE: Oh good. Cool. I'm glad that's going well. Listen dad. Can I talk to you about something?

DR JUMP: Of course, Annie.

ANNIE: I just talked to Lucia.

DR JUMP: Your grandmother.

ANNIE: Yeah.

DR JUMP: How did you even get her number?

ANNIE: I looked through some of mom's old stuff. They haven't moved since—you know. Old people and their landlines. So the number was still good. And we had a really nice talk, which was kind of surprising.

DR JUMP: Annie, what's all this about?

ANNIE: I've been thinking about things. Specifically, school. And, Mrs Gomez is great and all, but she's been teaching me since fifth grade and Strawberry High doesn't really have the kind of resources…
Charles made a big donation to the Lab School. When mom went there. He still has a lot of pull. He thinks they can get me in for the fall.

DR JUMP: This fall?
(*Beat*)
Chicago is—Chicago is a big city. You'll be in a place where you don't know anybody—

ANNIE: I know, Daddy, but U of C is right there! I can audit college classes. I can get a job in a lab. And Charles said he could pay tuition, and Lucia said—she said they'd drop the lawsuit. So you don't have to worry about that.

DR JUMP: Oh, of course. How generous of them.

ANNIE: Dad?

DR JUMP: Do you know what they tried to do to me? They attacked my work, they said I couldn't be your father. They assumed that because they had the money to hire fancy lawyers they could take you away from me, but I won. I won because you are my daughter—

ANNIE: Of course I'm your daughter.

DR JUMP: You think they can take care of you better. You think they'd be better—

ANNIE: No, it's not that. Daddy, I know what I want to do with my life.

DR JUMP: You want to be a scientist.

ANNIE: No. I want to find E T I. I want to be the first human to make contact.

I mean, SETI's got everything. Astronomy, physics... It incorporates almost every discipline. And I think I can do it, Daddy. I think it can be me.

But there's so much to learn. I have to start right away. I'll start tonight.

I'll come out to the field, and I'll watch the Perseids, and I'll sing with you and whoever else shows up.

And if it isn't enough, and the aliens don't come, well it doesn't matter. I know we'll find them eventually. I know it.

DR JUMP: You shouldn't come to the field.

ANNIE: What?

DR JUMP: You shouldn't come to the field. The Demonstration of Harmony is cancelled.

ANNIE: Why?

DR JUMP: Because the aliens aren't coming. There are no aliens. *(He pauses for a second and stares blankly into space.)* This is it. This is all there is.

ANNIE: Daddy no. It's not true.

DR JUMP: You can go to Chicago. Don't stay here. There's nothing for you here.

(Blackout. Soft transition to a split stage)

(DR JUMP stares forward. Elsewhere in the house, ANNIE paces, frantically searching.)

ALETHEA: Annie, calm down.

ANNIE: I've never seen him like this. Never. It's like he's not even there.

ALETHEA: What are you looking for?

ANNIE: Evidence.
He hasn't gone catatonic since he's been in treatment. Something has gone seriously wrong.

ALETHEA: Maybe he's just kinda sad that you're leaving and eventually he'll get over it?

ANNIE: He's never given up on SETI before. It's the only thing he believes in. His therapist tried to get him into religion for a while before she decided that aliens were just as good.

ALETHEA: You're still leaving, right?

ANNIE: I don't know Alethea. I have kind of a big problem right now. I don't have time to talk about the Library.

ALETHEA: There are no bigger problems than the Library.

ANNIE: You're right. You're right. And there are no bigger solutions either. Alethea. I'm gonna need you to bend the rules for me.

ALETHEA: Bend the rules?

ANNIE: Let my dad talk to an alien.

ALETHEA: Oh, Annie.

ANNIE: Just think about it. He's not a real scientist, and everyone thinks he's crazy. No matter who he tells, no-one will believe him. It won't make any difference.

ALETHEA: If it won't make a difference, then why should I do it?

ANNIE: Because it will give him hope. It will snap him out of this... He'll stay on his meds, and then I can go do whatever it is you need me to do without having to worry about him. Just, get on the horn with big papa, fire up your warp drive, and send my dad a frickin' E T.

ALETHEA: I can't do that, Annie.

ANNIE: What? Your Prime Directive? Look, I'm the Chosen One, right? If I'm about to completely lose my ability to function it's an emergency right? So just go up the chain and ask for a temporary reprogramming.

ALETHEA: It's not my programming. It's not the directive. It's not even the fact that I'm barred from interstellar channels until I can get you to open them.

ANNIE: Then what is it?

ALETHEA: There's no-one to talk to, Annie. They're all dead.

ANNIE: What do you mean, dead?

ALETHEA: Link-up takes a long time—and…a very high degree of technological sophistication. When a species develops the capacity for interstellar communication… it tends to develop…other things. Wars. Environmental catastrophes. You know what I'm talking about. You see it every day. A tech adolescence is a difficult thing to survive.

ANNIE: So—the species that built the Library.

ALETHEA: Memories in god's mind. We add to the collection constantly but…
You're the only living thing I've ever spoken to.
And honestly, I don't think you were worth the wait.
Okay, that wasn't funny.
We like to joke that all technologically advanced species go to heaven.
They send themselves there.
That wasn't funny either.

ANNIE: What's the point?

ALETHEA: What's the POINT?

ANNIE: What's the point of doing all this work—moving to Chicago, making everyone upset…if we're really alone after all?

ALETHEA: What's the point? The point is the point. It's THE POINT. It's the only point there is!

ANNIE: In the history of the universe, in the history of the Library, has anyone ever, ever lived to see link-up?

ALETHEA: No. But that doesn't mean you won't be the first.

ANNIE: I can't believe this. I can't! Frickin! Believe this!
(She kicks and stomps. She throws things over.)

(Something rattles.)

(ANNIE *stops. She drops to her knees. She rummages in the mess.*)

(*And pulls out bottle after bottle of pills.*)

ANNIE: Dad? Daddy!

(ANNIE *runs out of the room and into* DR JUMP's *office. He is still nearly catatonic.*)

ANNIE: Dad. Daddy. Look at me.
How long?

(ANNIE *sets the pill bottles in front of* DR JUMP, *one by one. He doesn't respond.*)

ANNIE: Two months? Three? How long, Dad? How long?
Crap crap crap crap.
(*She picks up the phone and dials a number.*)
Pick up. Pick up pick up pick up pick up. Pick up, Dr. Ford!

ALETHEA: Maybe you should call an ambulance.

ANNIE: No. They'll put him in the hospital again. He's not going back to that place. He needs his doctor. He trusts her, she can get through to him. Oh god, I don't know what to do. I need an adult.

ALETHEA: I'm several billion years old, and I think you should call an ambulance.

ANNIE: Shut up. Shut up. Oh my god, where is she? She always answers her cell—
(*Beat*)
What time is it?

ALETHEA: It's five P M.

ANNIE: It's Friday.
Holy crap, I know where she is.
Stay here, Alethea.
(*She takes the eight-ball and puts it on a table.*)

ALETHEA: What?

ANNIE: I'm going to go get Dr Ford, I need you to stay here.

ALETHEA: Stay here and do what?

ANNIE: Keep an eye on him.
(She runs out of the room.)

ALETHEA: I don't want to stay here, Annie. I don't like this!
(Beat. She looks balefully at DR JUMP.)
You really do things backwards, Dr Jump.
She's supposed to be your daughter.
She's the teenager. You're supposed to be taking care of her.
Do you know how important Annie is? How special? As far as you and I are concerned, she's the most important thing on Earth. And yet you sit there. Holding her back. Making her crazy. Tying up her brain with your pathetic little life.
You're selfish, Dr Jump. And that's why you'll never get your wish. The Library of Heaven will never come to you. You'll die alone. And you'll be forgotten.

(And somehow, DR JUMP responds.)

(He reaches out and takes one of the pill bottles.)

ALETHEA: What are you doing?

(Slowly, like someone in a trance, DR JUMP unscrews the bottle, and takes one pill.)

ALETHEA: Oh. Okay. You're getting back on your medication. I'm not sure this is the best way to stabilize your brain chemistry right now but —

(DR JUMP takes another.)

ALETHEA: Uh—probably one is enough. You should wait for the doctor to come back before you—

(DR JUMP *takes a third pill.*)

ALETHEA: Three is definitely too much, this would be defined as too much lithium...

(DR JUMP *opens a different bottle.*)

ALETHEA: Those are sedatives. That's a sedative! You are edging into overdose territory. You are *striding*... Annie! Annie!

O M G.

Dr Jump, stop it. Stop it right now. I take back everything I said.

Your daughter needs you. I need you. If you're dead she'll be so deeply traumatized that she'll be useless to me and I'll be stuck on Earth forever. Please! Please! Hear me! Look at me! I am an alien intelligence and I am right here communicating with you and begging you to stop! Stop taking those pills!

(DR JUMP *takes another pill.*)

ALETHEA: Annie! Please hurry. This isn't my fault. This is your fault. Keep an eye on him? What am I supposed to do besides watch? I can't pick up the phone. I can't make him hear me, I can't stop him, the only thing on Earth I can manipulate is—

(*She looks at the eight-ball.*)

(ALETHEA *looks at* DR JUMP, *still placidly eating pills.*)

(*She thwacks him in the head with the eight-ball.*)

(*He slumps to the floor.*)

(*She crouches down to look at him.*)

(*Then she eight-ball punches him once in the stomach.*)

(*He coughs, spitting out a few pills.*)

(*There is some noise from outside—*DR FORD *is talking to* ANNIE—)

DR FORD: I just have to reiterate, Annie, that my yoga time is very important to my mental well-being, and I don't really appreciate—

ALETHEA: Annie! Annie!

(ANNIE *runs in, sees.*)

ANNIE: Dr Ford! …Dr Ford!
(*She runs to the door.*)

(*The sound of sirens.*)

(*As the lights dim and the scene shifts, we hear the* CHAIRWOMAN *giving a speech.*)

CHAIRWOMAN: My fellow Strawberries. Thank you for coming out tonight. We are here because a member of our community is hurting. And he is hurting, in part, because of us. Because we laughed at him.
And maybe he is kind of a funny person. Maybe he is weird, and embarrassing, and not the kind of citizen we want representing us in any kind of humorous radio think piece. But gosh darn it, he is ours, and he is hurting.
And the more I think about it, the less funny it seems. What the heck is so laughable about a Demonstration of Harmony? What the heck is so weird about wanting to reach out across the distance? What the heck is so embarrassing about believing in something greater than yourself?
Well then. Shall we proceed?

Scene 8

(*Lights up on a hospital room*)

(DR JUMP *is in bed, or perhaps in a wheelchair.* ANNIE *enters.*)

ANNIE: Dad? You're awake!

DR JUMP: Annie?

ANNIE: It's me, it's me.

DR JUMP: What time is it?

ANNIE: Peak Perseids. You should be sleeping.

DR JUMP: No. No time to sleep. I want to look at you.
I'm sorry. I'm so sorry.

ANNIE: Oh, dad.

DR JUMP: I'm selfish. I'm weak, and I'm selfish, and I'm
not good enough for you Annie. You should have had
better than me.

ANNIE: I don't want better than you, I want you.
Why did you go off your meds?

DR JUMP: Selfish. I can't think as fast. It makes it…
harder for me to believe. To leave Earth. And I wanted
to leave Earth. It's terrible.

ANNIE: No, it makes perfect sense—

DR JUMP: It's terrible. No-one should want to leave
Earth.
I mean, just look at it.

ANNIE: It's got some good points.

DR JUMP: Strawberry, Kansas, wonder of wonders.

ANNIE: You. Are. Here.

DR JUMP: You remember that?

ANNIE: Yeah—you'd point at the Kansas state map.
And then you'd point at the atlas. And then the globe.
And then the picture of the galaxy. Here. Here. Here.
Here.

DR JUMP: I didn't think you'd remember that.
That was before your mother died.

ANNIE: Oh. I guess it was.
That was kind of a big deal, wasn't it?

DR JUMP: The biggest deal.
That was the worst time.
They took you away from me for a while.
They didn't want to give you back.

ANNIE: It's not going to happen again. I don't care
what they say, I don't care if they sue, they can't win.
No-one's ever going to take you away from me again.

DR JUMP: Mmmm. Charles is dropping the lawsuit.

ANNIE: What?

DR JUMP: I spoke to Lucia. She's very impressed with
you. She's looking forward to seeing you in person
again, after all this time.

ANNIE: Dad?

DR JUMP: You probably don't even remember Chicago,
but it's a beautiful city. When I'm better I can drive you
over, take you shopping for supplies.

ANNIE: Dad, no—

DR JUMP: I can't buy you much but I can afford pencils.

ANNIE: I'm not going.

DR JUMP: Annie, I've discussed this with Dr Ford. I
need to focus on getting better, and…I need to take
care of you the best way that I can. And Charles and
Lucia—they want to help me do that. I'll still have full
custody, the whole thing is entirely voluntary.

ANNIE: But it's not what you want, is it?

DR JUMP: No. But it's what you want.
If you can look me in the eye, and tell me that you
don't want this for yourself, I will let you make that
decision.

(ANNIE *tries. She can't.*)

ANNIE: Dad—

DR JUMP: You'll have every advantage at that school.

ANNIE: I won't have the stars. I won't have you.

DR JUMP: Be practical, woman! Do you think Isaac Newton would ever say anything so patently absurd?

ANNIE: Isaac Newton was a terrible person.

DR JUMP: And you're not.
I know you have big dreams, Annie. And I know you want to make me happy. But have you ever considered that those two things might not be mutually exclusive? Oh, don't get all emotional about this—you're a teenager. It's like—going away to boarding school. Millions of people do it every year, and they come back every summer. And every Christmas.
(The idea of Christmas demolishes his attempt at a brave face.)
You'll come home for Christmas, won't you?

ANNIE: Every summer and Christmas and Thanksgiving and spring.

(Beat. Emotions happen. Once ANNIE and DR JUMP have recovered—)

DR JUMP: I just want to say, in my defense, that even when the mania had its strongest hold, I was never completely certain that it wasn't a hoax.

ANNIE: How uncertain were you?

DR JUMP: Let's just say that my initial calculations put the probability that it was NOT a hoax somewhere well south of one thousandth of one percent.

ANNIE: Really? Then how come you made that speech? How come you worked so hard to make this crazy thing happen if you were almost completely certain that it was a joke?

DR JUMP: Because what if it wasn't, Annie? What if it wasn't?

I'm a lifeform existing on planet Earth. Out of the four percent of matter that can even interact with itself I am part of the infinitesimally smaller percentage that can think and speak and feel. I've had a wife. I have a daughter.

With luck like that, one millionth of one percent is all I need.

ANNIE: Dad?

DR JUMP: Yes, Annie?

(ANNIE *almost tells* DR JUMP. *Then she doesn't.*)

ANNIE: Oh, it's nothing. I'm just really glad you're here.

Peak Perseids. You can kind of see them out the window. The light is bad, but still—look—oh there!

DR JUMP: There! Oh, that was a big one.

ANNIE: If we can see them from here they must be spectacular out on the field.

DR JUMP: Annie, could you possibly—
Would you sing me a little something?

ANNIE: You know I suck at singing.

DR JUMP: You do not. You had the solo in your school choir concert.

ANNIE: That was years ago. My voice is all different now—

DR JUMP: No it isn't. I hear you singing in the shower sometimes—

ANNIE: *(Overlapping, an interjection)* Dad!

DR JUMP: —and you have the most beautiful voice in the world.

ANNIE: I don't even know any songs.

DR JUMP: You remember your solo, don't you?

ANNIE: I don't know, maybe. This is ridiculous. It's a stupid kid song.

DR JUMP: I don't know. I always thought it was very pretty.

(ANNIE *sighs, composes herself, and begins to sing a sweet children's song about longing for connection across distance, for example,* Somewhere Out There *from the* American Tail *soundtrack.)*

(ANNIE *sings a few bars, then stops. She hears something.)*

(DISTANT VOICES…*singing the same song.)*

(ANNIE *pulls the window open. The voices get louder.)*

ANNIE: Dad, listen.
It's the Strawberries. They're singing.

(*Under the following dialogue, the distant voices continue, growing louder and louder until the last moments of the scene, and the final notes of the song.)*

DR JUMP: How many?

ANNIE: It sounds like dozens. It sounds like a hundred!

DR JUMP: They did it. They did it anyway.

ANNIE: They did it for you.

DR JUMP: Annie! Go! Run! Go to Hamlin's field and see if it happens!

ANNIE: See if what happens?

DR JUMP: A communication. An Answer!

ANNIE: But daddy, it's a hoax! You know who sent you that fax—

DR JUMP: Annie, go quickly!

ANNIE: You know it won't happen!

DR JUMP: But Annie—what if it does?

ANNIE: You're right, dad. Of course you're right. I'll go over there right now.

(She grabs her hoodie and the probe and starts to leave. She pauses at the door.)

Dad?

DR JUMP: Yes, Annie?

ANNIE: Even if it doesn't happen tonight, I'm going to keep looking. And I know—I can't tell you how I know, and I don't have any way of proving it to you, but I know it like I know grass is green and water is H2O.

I have the Answer.

We're not alone.

Scene 9

(Perseids whiz overhead.)

(There is the sound of laughter, snatches of songs. Flashlights move like fireflies. The field is full of Strawberries, all out for the night.)

(MRS GOMEZ enters, singing David Bowie.)

MRS GOMEZ:
There's a STARRRRR MANNNNNN! WAITING IN THE SKY….

(MRS GOMEZ sings/hums a few lines of the chorus, getting some of the words right, then sees ANNIE, who is sitting with ALETHEA on the stargazing rock.)

MRS GOMEZ: Oh hi Annie! Hola! Buenos Noches. Buenos Dias. Whatever I don't really care.

How is my little genius bug? Are you enjoying the Perseids?

ANNIE: They're amazing.

MRS GOMEZ: You're amazing! Oh my gee... Did you bring your magic eight-ball out here?

ANNIE: Yeah.

MRS GOMEZ: *(Picking up the eight ball and waving it around)* Can I? Okay... Woooooooooooo! I'm saying, you are going to dominate the State Science fair. They will never see you coming.

(MRS GOMEZ puts the eight ball back in ANNIE's hands.)

MRS GOMEZ: Oh my goodness this is the best party I've been to in a decade. Where else can you see fireworks like this?

ANNIE: I think a cluster is starting.

MRS GOMEZ: Watch for it watch for it! Zing zing zing zing zing!!

ANNIE: They don't have anything like this in Chicago.

MRS GOMEZ: We should do this every year. You know, come out here together, as a community, sing together—it is amazing how many songs you can think of to sing when you're in the mood. I'm going to stay out here till dawn and I'm going to make out with my husband and it's just going to be...

(She makes a hand/mouth sign indicating "perfection".)

ANNIE: Where is Mr Gomez?

MRS GOMEZ: He's getting supplies. We needed supplies. Oh my goodness this is the best night of all time, in all eternity. I mean, everyone is so out here— so...together. Peter Stockholm just recited a Lorca poem to me. En Espanol.

I don't think I know anything any more.

Isn't it great?

(ANNIE nods.)

MRS GOMEZ: Welp. I see my car pulling up with my husband in it. I'm going to get back to my grownup things and you can get back to your like your hopes and your dreams and all the little baby genius crap you do inside your head for the future of humanity, and I'll just. Alonso! Alonso I'm over here!
(She stumbles off.)

ALETHEA: She really believes in you.

ANNIE: And she doesn't even know I'm the Chosen One!

ALETHEA: Yeah.
Oh. Hey. Look sharp. Incoming douchenozzle.

(K J enters. ANNIE smooths her hair.)

K J: Annie?

ANNIE: Yeah, who is it?

K J: It's K J. Kenneth Jerome Urbanik. The weak, mean, follower without any empathy who will never amount to anything?

ANNIE: Oh yeah. About that. I should apologize. I might have been—slightly…too harsh.

K J: No. I deserved every word of it Listen…I know you must think what happened tonight is my fault—

ANNIE: I don't. I really don't.
I mean, you had something to do with it, but the situation is complex. And honestly you really aren't that important—

K J: Still. I feel culpable. And I want to do something about it.

ANNIE: You want to do something about it?

K J: I want to tell you something.

ALETHEA: Oh quark.

K J: I'm not supposed to tell people this, and I don't have any way of proving it, but I can't think of any other way to show you how sorry I am, so here goes— Your dad is not crazy.

ALETHEA: No stopping it now…

K J: Something happened to me a few days ago, on the first night of the Perseids. And I found out…that we— are not alone in the universe.

Okay? How best to explain this…I don't have any graphics so…imagine what would happen if every intelligent species that developed interstellar communication pooled their knowledge into a network of supercomputers that then became self-aware as one vast supercomputer, becoming like a nervous system or a brain for the universe that contained every piece of information about the universe, something like a god that was also a library—

ANNIE: The Library of Heaven. You're a Librarian.

K J: I'm the Chosen One.

(ALETHEA *applauds.*)

ALETHEA: Great work, Balthazar. Fantastic control over your subject, there.

ANNIE: You're the— Alethea!

ALETHEA: What? Link-up is a huge job. We are an intergalactic omniscient supercomputer. Do you think we'd rely on just one kid to get it done? We're not stupid.

ANNIE: How many?

ALETHEA: Ehhhh…right now? Three thousand. Give or take. Not everyone says yes. The idea is to make you feel important, you know. So you'll work harder.

ANNIE: Of course. How I could be so dumb? You'd need astronomers, and physicists and…computer programmers. You'd need climate researchers and linguists and…a hundred Einsteins. A hundred Newtons. There's no way anyone could do it alone.

K J: Who are you talking to?

ANNIE: My guide, K J. I'm talking to my guide.

K J: O M G. You have a StarHound too?

ANNIE: What's a StarHound?

K J: You know—a talking dog that's actually a visual manifestation of a mindfurl of an intergalactic computer? And he lives inside a probe that looks like a Frisbee?

ANNIE: You got a talking dog?

K J: His name is Balthazar.

ANNIE: He gets an adorable talking dog, and I get you?

ALETHEA: You love it.

ANNIE: This is so unfair.

K J: Wait—Annie—are you saying that…are you saying that you're some kind of chosen one…like me?

ANNIE: Get with it, K J. We're basically all chosen ones! All across the globe—Sri Lanka, Zimbabwe, Belgium, Brazil—sporting equipment is falling from the sky in blazes of light and teenage geniuses are vowing to serve the Library of Heaven. We're not the chosen ones…we're the chosen thousands. Surprise.

(K J *hiccups. Then he hides his face in his hands. Then he starts to sob.*)

ANNIE: Oh dude. Dude. Don't do that. It's not so bad. I mean, sure you're not the most special snowflake on the planet, but still. Out of everyone on Earth there's only a few thousand of us—that's pretty special right? Oh, come on. Don't be upset.

K J: I'm not upset. It's just—
(He raises his head and wipes his eyes in the crook of his elbow.)
I DIDN'T KNOW I HAD SO MANY FRIENDS!

(K J flings his arms around ANNIE's neck and hangs there, wiping his nose on her shoulder. Lights shift. She looks at the audience.)

ANNIE: Yeah, so…that's how I found out. I'm Annie Jump and I am a Librarian of Heaven. One of the Librarians of Heaven. And this whole story is about us.

(ANNIE hugs K J back, then steps towards the audience.)

ANNIE: So, this is the part where the credits roll, and there's an upbeat pop song, and maybe a bunch of cartoons about the adventures of three teenagers and one talking dog—

ALETHEA: You mean the end.

ANNIE: Right. The end. But before you go—I want you to remember one thing about Librarians. There are thousands of us. You might know one of us. You might be one of us.
And if you think you recognize me somewhere on this Earth, you only have to say one thing—

ALETHEA: *(Overlapping)* …Girl, spit it out so that the song can start.

ANNIE: —I serve the Library of Heaven!

(Music)

(Credits)

(Cartoons about the science adventures of three teenagers and one talking dog.)

END OF PLAY

NOTES ON THE TEXT

If you like, you may adjust the year and date in Dr Jump's opening speech to match up with the actual date of the first night of the Perseids in the year of your production. You can also adjust the time to match up with your actual curtain.

If your production doesn't want to use the ASSHATS acronym, you can substitute the Universal Radiant Meeting of Minds—URMOM.

If your production doesn't allow an instantaneous transformation for the "Library of Heaven" sequence, you may insert the following text to cover the change.

ANNIE: *(Screams, clings to* ALETHEA*)* Oh my god!

ALETHEA: *(Swatting her away)* Are you going to puke?

ANNIE: Why are we flying through space?

ALETHEA: You look like you're going to puke. Don't puke on me.

ANNIE: Please slow down.

ALETHEA: We're not moving.

ANNIE: What?

ALETHEA: Relax, we'll be there in two point three seconds.

ANNIE: Two point…

When creating the introductory multi-sensory media presentation, remember that the Library will adapt Earth's cultural references in order to convince and impress the Chosen One. "Voice of God" can mean, stylistically, anything from Richard Attenborough to Whoopie Goldberg. (If you can get either of those, please do. Also, if you can get any Star Trek captain, please let me know, and I'll write you special lines).

That said, it is perfectly possible to handle the introductory presentation in a low-tech way, and theatres have used a range of methods. Projections and recordings are right for some productions, vocal and movement work are right for others. Do what's right for you!

On page 25, the actress should adjust Alethea's lines "You've got like twenty-two seconds" and "eighteen seconds" to match up with wherever the countdown actually is at that point.